TROUBLE

HELEN CRESSWELL

illustrated by Margaret Chamberlain

LONDON   VICTOR GOLLANCZ LTD   1987

*To Maisie Daisy Rosie Posy Ousbey Lousbey
With love,*
H.C.

ESSEX COUNTY LIBRARY

First published in Great Britain 1987
by Victor Gollancz Ltd
14 Henrietta Street, London WC2E 8QJ

Text copyright © Helen Cresswell 1987
Illustrations copyright © Margaret Chamberlain 1987

British Library Cataloguing in Publication Data
Cresswell, Helen
　Trouble.
　　I. Title   II. Chamberlain, Margaret
　823'.914[J]　　　PZ7

ISBN 0-575-04035-1

Printed in Hong Kong by Imago Publishing Limited

EJ 63659

Emma Golightly was five years old and nearly six. She lived with her mother (whose name was Lizzie) and her dog, Boots, whom she liked to pretend was her brother. Boots was as good as gold (at least that's what Mum always said).

Emma Golightly, alas, was not as good as gold. She didn't even *want* to be. She wanted to find out what was on the other side of walls and fences. This meant climbing up them,

and sometimes scuffing her shoes or tearing her jeans. This meant trouble.

She wanted to find out what was in the big blue jug on the top shelf of the dresser. This meant climbing on a chair and things somehow being knocked off the shelf and broken. This meant trouble.

She always wanted to stay to the very end of games of hide and seek. This meant she was often late for tea. This meant trouble.

"Why can't you be like Boots?" Mum would sigh. "Look at him—good as gold!"

Sometimes Emma Golightly felt that she would scream if Mum said that one more time.

Then, one day, Gran was coming to stay. Gran was quite old and wore hats and was always knitting, and Emma loved her. Gran lived in a village a long way off, so Mum and Emma and Boots set off in the car to fetch her.

When they arrived Gran had her hat on ready to go and sat knitting.

"This is for you," she told Emma. "It's a jumper."

"So you must be sure to look after it," Mum said,

" and not get it dirty, or tear it. When *I* was a little girl, I looked after my clothes."

"Stuff and nonsense!" said Gran.

They stared at her.

"When *you* were a little girl, Lizzie," Gran told her, "your clothes would be dirty not five minutes after you'd put them on!"

"Really?" Emma was amazed.

"Really," nodded Gran. "I'd sometimes have to change her clothes three times a day."

"Well, I don't remember that!" said Mum, who had gone pink.

"Now come along, let's go!"

But Gran took no notice.

"I remember one particular day, Lizzie," she went on. "First you climbed up the apple tree and tore your best skirt. Then you spilt tomato sauce all down your frock, and *then* you went tadpoling and fell in the pond! You came home looking like a waterfall. A *muddy* waterfall!"

Emma beamed at Gran, and Gran beamed back.

"I think I'm ready now, Lizzie," she said, putting away her knitting.

So off they went, and all the way home Emma was very quiet. She was trying to picture Mum up an apple tree, or toppling into a pond full of tadpoles.

When they got home Gran had a present each for Emma and Boots. She gave Boots a bone and Emma a musical box that played *Home Sweet Home*. Boots gnawed his bone.

Emma went behind the sofa to try to find out where the music came from. She did find out, in the end, but by then the box was broken. It was just a plain, ordinary box without music.

It wasn't long before Mum found out.

"You're a naughty girl!" she told Emma. "When *I* was a little girl, I looked after my presents!"

"Rubbish!" said Gran.

They stared at her.

"When *you* were a little girl, Lizzie," Gran told her, "you broke more presents than I've had hot dinners! Jack-in-the-boxes, dolls that cry, clockwork mice – you broke them all!"

"Did you, Mum?" said Emma, enchanted.

"I remember in particular a beautiful doll your Aunt Mary give you one Christmas," went on Gran. "It didn't last five minutes. First you poked its open-and-shut eyes right inside its head, and then you fetched the scissors and cut off all its beautiful gold hair. Bald as a coot that doll was when you'd done with it, and blind as a bat!"

"I don't remember," said Mum.

"But I do," said Gran. She beamed at Emma, and Emma beamed back.

"I have just remembered," said Gran. "I bought another present for Emma." It was a big kite, with a long tail.

"We'll go for a picnic, this afternoon," said Mum. "Then you can fly it."

So they went to a high, windy hill, and soon the kite was flying. Emma held the string and it tugged and pulled as if it were alive. Then, all of a sudden, the string slipped through her fingers and had gone!

"Help!" cried Emma. "Come back!"
But the kite went soaring away like a bird, over the hill, over the treetops and out of sight.
Emma started to cry.

"Fancy losing that lovely kite, Emma!" said Mum. "I really don't know! When *I* was a little girl, I never lost things."

"Fiddlesticks!" said Gran.

They stared at her.

"I never knew such a child for losing things as you were, Lizzie," Gran went on. "You started when you were still in your pram! Rattles, woolly bunnies, mitts, teething rings—over the side they went, all of them!"

Emma stopped crying, and instead tried to imagine Mum as a baby in a pram, tossing things over the edge in a shower. Whatever would Gran say next?

"Come and help me pack up the things," said Mum hastily.
"On the way home, I'd like you to stop at a shop that sells ice cream, Lizzie," Gran said.
"I shall buy one for Emma."

"Oh, do you think you should, so soon after tea?" said Mum. "When *I* was a—" She stopped.

"Yes, Lizzie?" said Gran sweetly.
 "Oh—nothing!" Mum said.
 Gran beamed at Emma, and Emma beamed back.